IMAGES
of America

SYMPHORIA
THE ORCHESTRA OF
CENTRAL NEW YORK

ON THE COVER: Music director Lawrence Loh leads Symphoria and the audience in the national anthem at a season-opening concert. (Courtesy of Marc Ramos.)

IMAGES
of America

SYMPHORIA
THE ORCHESTRA OF
CENTRAL NEW YORK

Barbara Sheklin Davis
Foreword by Peter J. Rabinowitz

ARCADIA
PUBLISHING

Published by Arcadia Publishing
Charleston, South Carolina

Printed in the United States of America

Library of Congress Control Number: 2022942036

For all general information, please contact Arcadia Publishing:
Telephone 843-853-2070
Fax 843-853-0044
E-mail sales@arcadiapublishing.com
For customer service and orders:
Toll-Free 1-888-313-2665

Visit us on the Internet at www.arcadiapublishing.com

*To my husband, Leslie, who loved, composed, and played
music, and to the Symphoria musicians and supporters
who share his passion for the orchestral repertoire*

CONTENTS

FOREWORD

At first, this book might seem of purely local concern. What larger interest could there be in the history of an orchestra in a smallish Central New York city? In fact, though, this volume might well have been titled *The Triumph of Sisyphus*—and it can serve as inspiration for a much wider audience.

Sisyphus, you will remember, was the mythological Greek king who was condemned for eternity to roll a heavy rock up a hill, only to have it repeatedly fall back. When the Syracuse Symphony went bankrupt in 2011, during its 50th anniversary season, many in the community felt like Sisyphus, caught in an endless cycle of futility. After all, since the late 19th century, many local orchestras had been organized, only to roll down into the heap of the city's "former" orchestras.

This time, though, something different happened. Yes, yet another orchestra, eventually named Symphoria, was founded. But this one was created by the players themselves. Fueled by their tenacious love of music and guided by their idealism, they rejected the traditional administrative structure that had led to so many disappointments in the past. Instead, they formed a cooperative that bypassed the usual board/player conflicts and gave them a sense of ownership in the organization.

The results? As you might expect from an orchestra made up of players who are willing to make personal sacrifices to keep music alive in their community, Symphoria has maintained the highest standards of both artistic integrity and artistic flexibility (especially valuable during the pandemic, as changing health regulations led to last-minute alterations in programming). At the same time, the cooperative spirit has stimulated the orchestra to integrate itself into the life of the community—to reflect, through its repertoire, the larger community of Syracuse; to collaborate with community-service organizations; and to participate in a wide range of community events and educational activities.

In sum, Symphoria is not only a success but also a model. As we watch orchestras struggling across the country, it is well worth paying attention to the story Barbara Sheklin Davis tells here.

—Peter J. Rabinowitz

ACKNOWLEDGMENTS

This book would not have been possible without the generous access provided by Marc Ramos to his wonderful photographic archives and without the knowledge, guidance, and assistance of Symphoria's Lawrence Loh, Jon Garland, Peter Rabinowitz, and especially Pamela Murchison. Thanks are due also to Vicki Feldman, Gregg Tripoli of the Onondaga Historical Association, and Henry Fogel and the staff of the local history section of the Onondaga Public Library.

   Unless otherwise noted, all images appear courtesy of Marc Ramos.

INTRODUCTION

With tongue in cheek, a music critic suggested that the way orchestras could stop losing money was to stop performing concerts. He reasoned that since orchestras can only recoup 50–70 percent of their expenses through ticket sales, leaving the shortfall to be covered by monarchs, governments, or philanthropists, by failing to perform, they could reduce their deficits. He further suggested that instead of having an orchestra perform in concert with a soloist, it would be better to just have a soloist, who would be paid less than the full orchestra. At this point, his suggestions ceased being amusing.

Yet the problem of orchestras and their funding is crucial to the continuance of orchestral music, not only in America but throughout the world. It is estimated that there are between 1,200 and 1,700 symphony orchestras in the United States. Finances are always a primary concern. As Robert J. Flanagan writes in *The Perilous Life of Symphony Orchestras*, "Orchestras must rely upon income that does not flow from their normal operations."

The story of Symphoria, the orchestra of Central New York, which is celebrating with exuberance its 10th anniversary in 2022, is the story of orchestral triumph over repeated financial disaster. Symphoria arose like a phoenix from the ashes of its predecessor, the Syracuse Symphony Orchestra (SSO), which, in turn, arose from multiple predecessors of the same name that were born, flourished, and died within the prior century.

What makes a community want an orchestra? What makes a community want an orchestra over and over again? Support for an orchestra in Syracuse waxed and waned for 100 years but was never extinguished. The financial issues common to all orchestras, however, seem to have been endemic to all iterations of the Syracuse Symphony, and the burden for generating support was repeatedly placed upon the musicians themselves. Even as early a work as Dwight H. Bruce's 1891 *Memorial History of Syracuse, N.Y., from Its Settlement to the Present Time* identified the problem. In a description of the state of the orchestral music situation of his day, Bruce presciently wrote, "Efforts to permanently establish choral societies and orchestras have repeatedly failed and such experiences must continue until the time shall come when musicians shall generally join their efforts in a common cause." Thirty years later, another SSO originator, Henri De Pavoloff, echoed the sentiment, saying, "It is only a question of waking people up to the necessity. We musicians must all work together to educate the people's musical appetites."

In all, there were five musical ensembles bearing the name Syracuse Symphony Orchestra before Symphoria was formed. Perhaps the new name and new mission, vision, and values of Symphoria will allow it to succeed where its predecessors did not. Symphoria differs from its predecessors in significant ways. Jon Garland, a musician who was one of the leaders in the struggle to create the new entity, explained, "There were all sorts of different ideas about what a new orchestra might look like. The musicians had a path that they thought was good, the university had a path, and there were others who had different ideas. Symphoria is a result of all those groups coming together and agreeing on a single way forward for a professional orchestra in Syracuse."

As a musician-owned and -governed organization, Symphoria is on the cutting edge of the business model for American orchestras. The relationship between the board and the artistic director is more collaborative than is the norm with most other orchestras. Music director Lawrence Loh actively seeks ways to partner with other arts organizations in the city. "We all coexist, and we all have the same mission," he says, "trying to work to enrich lives through great art." Symphoria's 50 musicians own a part of the orchestra and contribute to its development and operation. Board and orchestra member Jon Garland adds, "Sometimes, in a traditional orchestra, if there is not full transparency between different components of the organization, there can be distrust. When we arrived at this structure, we didn't want to go back to that."

Symphoria is a community organization, designed to connect members of the Syracuse community with orchestral and ensemble performances in diverse and accessible venues. It eschews elitism in favor of excellence, exclusion in favor of inclusion, declaring, "We strive to create an inclusive organization where all people—musicians, youth orchestra members, staff, board members, volunteers, and audience—feel they truly belong."

Symphoria promised to listen to and learn from Central New York's Black, Indigenous, people of color, and other underrepresented communities, allocating time and resources to achieve diverse, equitable, and inclusive representation within its board, staff, volunteers, orchestra, repertoire, audience, and guest artists. It committed itself to creating programs tied to community events and history that were relevant to diverse audiences in order to bring awareness to and celebrate the achievements, traditions, and cultures of all segments of the community. Its goal was to feature composers and musicians from underrepresented groups and present concerts and educational events to audiences of all traditions and backgrounds at the highest possible level of performance.

The desire to keep live symphonic music in Syracuse has had many proponents but also many failures. Symphoria's story is unique in that it demonstrates the ability of a dedicated community to prove that culture is not the sole province of one segment of society or of large cities; that young people crave and value musical education; and that dedication to diversity, equity, and inclusion can make orchestral music meaningful to people of many different backgrounds in the 21st century.

Symphoria: The Orchestra of Central New York describes the work of dedicated and idealistic community members for whom orchestral music expresses the deepest emotions and thoughts of civilization. It is the story of their commitment, trust, and belief that they would prevail, despite all obstacles, in offering Central New York the beauty, peace, and inspiration that orchestral music provides. The repeated creations, failures, and recreations of the symphony over the past decades prove the validity of a remark made by flutist John Oberbrunner after the orchestra's 14-week strike in 1983. Oberbrunner told a reporter, "There are a few pessimists who keep saying this community is too small. You can keep saying that, but miracles keep happening." The following pages recount those miracles.

One

OVERTURE

Orchestras were not part of the Syracuse musical scene until the end of the 19th century. Bands were. There were several dozen bands, fully outfitted in smart uniforms and representing a full spectrum of ethnic affiliations and instrumentation. There were those in the community, however, who sought a more elegant and serious form of musical performance. When the very first Syracuse Symphony Orchestra was formed in 1892, the *Syracuse Daily News* described the motivation for its creation: "The symphonic orchestra was organized for the purpose of elevating the musical standard of Syracuse and desires the support of the citizens."

That first pioneering orchestra, led first by Charles A. Ball and then by Albert Kuenzlen, lasted only two years before it was disbanded, but it introduced Syracuse to symphonic music played by local musicians. The flame, once lit, was hard to extinguish. Five years later, in 1897, Conrad L. Becker, director of the violin department at Syracuse University, formed an orchestra with students from the university, several professors, and a number of local musicians. His goals were to provide the players an opportunity to study and perform the best compositions and to stimulate public interest in orchestral music. Becker managed the orchestra and kept the books in addition to his university duties. But after two years, unable to establish a business committee or generate financial support, this orchestra also disbanded.

The 20th century saw the formation of three other Syracuse Symphonies. In 1900, Syracuse University professor Gastin Berch conducted an orchestra also calling itself the Syracuse Symphony, but the orchestra was not ultimately a success. In 1909, Conrad Becker returned to the scene with the creation of yet another 40-member Syracuse Symphony Orchestra. A local music critic predicted that this SSO was "destined to play a considerable part in the local development of musical art in Syracuse," but, alas, its life was also short. In 1914, yet another Syracuse Symphony Orchestra, led by bandleader Patrick Conway of the Ithaca Conservatory of Music, gave several concerts at the Lincoln Auditorium of Central High School but soon faded into oblivion.

Dwight H. Bruce in his *Memorial History of Syracuse, N.Y., from Its Settlement to the Present Time*, published in 1891, was unflinching in his description of the state of music in the city: "The development of the art of music in Syracuse constitutes a subject which is not fruitful of important facts." He lamented the lack of an organized musical presence, writing that "to make a sketch of the various societies and orchestras which have risen only to fall, would entail considerable labor no more agreeable than that of writing other histories of misfortune." Nonetheless, he had hope for the future: "Let us rather look to the present and future for the fulfillment of bright hopes and turn to the past only for teachings to help in the attainment of a degree of musical culture which shall give Syracuse a reputation throughout the land." The Syracuse Symphony Orchestra, organized by Eugene Melvin with Syracuse University professor Gastin Berch as first director and pictured on the stage of the Wieting Opera House after a concert in December 1907, was a step in fulfilling Bruce's hopes.

In July 1921, Melville Clark, president of the Clark Music Company, hired Henri de Pavoloff, a visiting violinist at the Syracuse University School of Music, to organize a symphony orchestra. Clark was the symphony's major donor and became its first president. Rehearsals began in August with 50 musicians, mostly itinerant players with traveling vaudeville acts plus some local businessmen. E.F. Albee, who owned the Keith Theater, donated his venue at no charge for the performances, which were held at noon on weekdays so that businessmen could attend on their lunch hour. Admission was 75¢, and the auditorium was always filled. Due to scheduling and personal conflicts, de Pavoloff was replaced after fewer than a dozen rehearsals, and composer William Berwald was hired to conduct. The first concert was played on January 21, 1922, under Berwald's baton.

"More than 3,000 persons greeted the new Syracuse symphony orchestra under the leadership of Dr. William Berwald of Syracuse University with unstinted enthusiasm at its first concert at Keith's yesterday," reported the Sunday edition of the *Post-Standard*. Although only two concerts were originally scheduled for the opening season, they proved so popular that five were played. The newspaper reported that "all of the seats were taken by 12 o'clock, and soon after, the standing room was exhausted. Never before has an offering by home talent attracted so large an audience." The paper continued: "The most sanguine were overjoyed by the result. Dr. Berwald was an inspired leader for the 60 players in the band, who provided every required instrument. The players were keenly interested in every detail of the performance." The reviewer then added, "There can be no doubt that sufficient material is available in Syracuse for a permanent symphony orchestra, and the quality of the initial performance demonstrated that in time it will have a place among the leading orchestras of the country."

Vladimir Shavitch, conductor of the Rochester Theatre Orchestra, was engaged as the Syracuse orchestra's next music director and conductor in 1924. When he came to Syracuse, it was the smallest city in the United States to have its own orchestra. Shavitch thought big. He cut a dashing figure but was a hard taskmaster. An article in the local paper said that he "constantly shouted directions, drilled difficult passages unmercifully and possessed a great deal of stamina." He brought prominent musicians as soloists to Syracuse, continued youth concerts, began pops concerts, and extended the regular season to 10 concerts per year. He also arranged for the orchestra to play in nearby cities such as Watertown and Rome. In his first five seasons, audiences totaled 147,500, and the children's concerts introduced 18,000 youngsters to the orchestral repertoire.

VLADIMIR
SHAVITCH,
Conductor of
the Syracuse
Symphony
Orchestra,
Who Is Now
Conducting the
Lamoureux
Orchestra in
Paris, With His
Wife and
Daughter.
(Times Wide
World Photo,
Paris Bureau.)

In the summer, Shavitch would tour Europe, guest conducting famous orchestras such as the London Symphony, the Paris Conservatoire Orchestra, and the Moscow, Madrid, and Berlin Symphonies. Everywhere he conducted, he identified himself as "conductor of the Syracuse Symphony" on his billings, thus putting the Syracuse Symphony Orchestra on the world musical map.

The orchestra's performances were held in Syracuse's movie theaters. A local music critic described the community's appetite for orchestral music, despite the lack of appropriate concert halls, writing, "We should be enjoying our musical fair in a well-appointed hall, large enough to allow 5,000 of us to sit down comfortably, and not coping down on Saturday noon in much the same way as we swallow a hasty lunch and rush back to the office without loss of time. And yet, such is the apparent determination of the community to support and enjoy its symphony, that not on a single occasion during the season has the management had cause to complain of lax attendance, but, on the contrary, bumper and overflowing audiences have been the rule." Because the movie venues were designed for other fare, however, concertgoers were urged to exit speedily when the applause died down so that matinees could begin on schedule: "It is of the utmost importance that the theatre be emptied as quickly as possible after each Symphony Concert so that Keith's afternoon performance may begin on time."

A board of 40 trustees, with nine officers, governed the orchestra. Financial challenges were evident from its inception. Melville Clark described the orchestra as having "no money in its treasury to start with, no endowment fund, and no backing of a single wealthy person." Some support for the orchestra came in the form of public donations and concert sponsorships. An editorial in the *Syracuse Sunday Herald American* exhorted the citizenry to "join without delay in giving the SSO the once conclusive proof of their willingness to support it. Adequate revenue must be secured and the time to begin is now." A women's committee was organized to raise funds, and wealthy patrons like Mrs. H. Winfield Chapin (Marie) and Melville Clark kept the orchestra going. Fund drives, benefit concerts, and symphony balls were held to generate the income to balance the budget that ticket sales alone could not provide.

The SSO was at the top of its game in the early 1920s. The board of directors was strong and supportive. The women's auxiliary helped to raise funds to keep the deficits at a manageable level. Although the orchestra still relied on Syracuse's movie theaters for performances, it was able to attract renowned artists to perform with it. Among the most prominent were Arthur Honegger, who was the orchestra's first guest conductor in 1924, and Sergei Prokofiev (above), who, in 1926, played his Concerto in C Major, a virtuoso piece that he performed frequently on wide-ranging concert tours throughout the United States.

By 1926, the Syracuse Symphony had incurred a sizeable debt. Questions were raised about the orchestra's expenditures. The orchestra musicians were paid only half what they earned in the theaters and motion picture houses, while Shavitch was paid $10,000 per year. There was no will to cut his salary, but neither was there a willingness to donate more money to cover it. Shavitch's policy of bringing in musicians from Rochester to play with the orchestra, saying that they knew the scores and could carry the Syracuse musicians along, caused further dissension. Detractors asked why the Syracuse Symphony and its conductor should not be abolished altogether and the Rochester Symphony invited to perform in Syracuse instead. The Great Depression of 1929 brought an end to the SSO's triumphal march. Despite the dismal financial situation of the country, Shavitch planned an extravagant music festival for May 1933 in which George Gershwin was to participate. The symphony's board was not sympathetic to his plans.

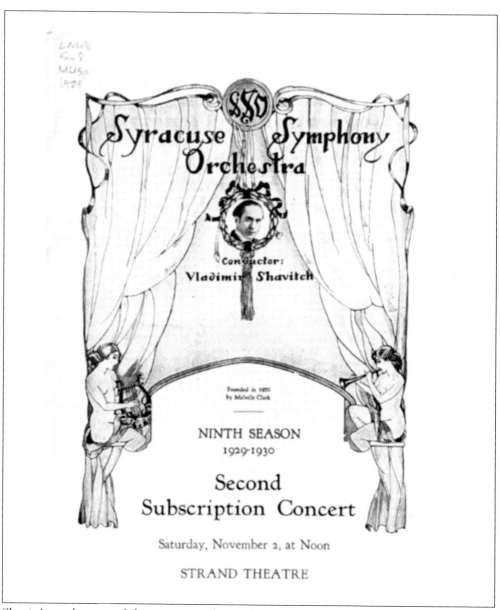

Syracuse Symphony Orchestra

Conductor:
Vladimir Shavitch

Founded in 1921
by Melville Clark

NINTH SEASON
1929-1930

Second
Subscription Concert

Saturday, November 2, at Noon

STRAND THEATRE

Shavitz's star began to fade as concern about a lack of funding grew and disagreement among board members about the wisdom of concertizing in a depression led to resignations and further financial losses. In 1932, Mrs. H. Winfield Chapin (Marie) resigned from the board. Whether she opposed Shavitz's choice of music and soloists or his extravagant spending was not clear. What was clear was that the local community was more concerned with getting itself out of the Depression than supporting musical events. The symphony's debts mounted as attendance dropped and patrons' support declined. The lack of financial support and poor attendance made it impossible for Shavitch to pay soloists after the first few concerts, and he left the community in 1933. At the end of its 12th season, the SSO board voted to dissolve the orchestra.

PICTURES FROM THE PAST

MEMBERS OF THE LONG BRANCH AMUSEMENT PARK OR-
CHESTRA IN 1898. Front row, left to right are H. Prowda,
Philip Mauer, F. Vermilea, E. Moss. Second row, H. Kenyon, F.
Comstock, Dr. Melfi. Rear row, Campbell, Eugene Melvin a n d
A. Drias

Several short-lived attempts at sustaining orchestral music in Syracuse occurred over the next
few years. The Civic Symphony Orchestra, sponsored by the City of Syracuse, was led by Victor
Miller and then by Andre Polah from 1933 to 1939. Renamed the Syracuse Federal Symphony,
it was supported by the New Deal's Works Progress Administration and was the only orchestra
that never had financial worries, as its federal funding covered all salary and related costs with no
need for local support. In 1940, having lost federal support due to the war effort, the orchestra was
again reorganized and renamed, becoming the Syracuse Symphony Orchestra Association. Two
other orchestras were also created: the Syracuse Philharmonic Society in 1942 and the Syracuse
Symphony Orchestra in 1949. During the 1940s and 1950s, other orchestras arose to fill the gap
left by the Syracuse Symphony, although most were repackagings of the same musicians under new
names: the Syracuse Civic Orchestra, the Civic University Orchestra, the Community Orchestra,
the Syracuse Symphony Society, and the Scottish Rite Symphony Orchestra. (Courtesy of the
Onondaga Historical Association.)

None of these ensembles survived for more than a few years, but the desire for symphonic music never wavered. There was always at least one orchestra during those decades, no matter how short-lived. The musicians remained devoted to the cause, although no conductor, according to music historian Susan Larson, "was dynamic enough to draw, keep, unify, and build up a devoted professional orchestra." Still, as Nicolas Gualillo, one of the era's conductors, wrote in a program note, the need for symphonic music was compelling: "In this day of the hydrogen bomb and the jet plane, the inspirational forces of man must not be neglected, for it is in the saving power of moral and cultural progress that we must look for the preservation of humanity." Gualillo was a violinist, composer, and instructor at the Utica Conservatory of Music. He made headlines when he resigned his position when *Salome's Dance of the Seven Veils* as interpreted by Thelma Biracree of the Eastman Music School's ballet department was banned by the Utica Civic Musical Society. Syracuse offered to host Biracree's performance. (Courtesy of the Onondaga Historical Association.)

Two

UNFINISHED SYMPHONY

A profusion of performing musical organizations was not a sustainable model, so in 1958, three groups consolidated as the Onondaga Symphony. Its first concert, with influential composer Lukas Foss as its guest conductor, was presented in 1959. In 1961, the Onondaga Symphony was offered a $50,000 grant from the Rosamond Gifford Foundation to hire a music director and business manager. The grant was given in support of a full concert season for adults and a continuation of the popular children's concerts. The orchestra's name was changed to the Syracuse Symphony Orchestra so that it was more closely identified with its city of origin. Thus was born the only Syracuse Symphony Orchestra that was destined to survive for decades.

The SSO became the 43rd largest orchestra in the United States. It performed classics, pops, and family series as well as educational programs and free summer park concerts. The orchestra operated two youth ensembles. The $6-million enterprise was supported through its volunteer organization, the Syracuse Symphony Association, and a 60-member board of directors.

The orchestra performed in Watertown, Rome, and Cortland; toured New York State; and performed in Delaware, Pennsylvania, New Hampshire, and Connecticut. It collaborated with Syracuse Opera, Syracuse Stage, the Syracuse University Oratorio Society, the Syracuse Children's Chorus, and the Syracuse School of Dance. It performed five times at Carnegie Hall, released recordings, and acquired a permanent home.

But even as the orchestra thrived on stage, things in the back office were not so stellar. The SSO was barely surviving financially. In 1983, the musicians went on strike for 14 weeks. In February 1992, the management cancelled four months of the season because it had no money. In 1998, there was another strike. The year 2006 was the last one the symphony was in the black. From then on, it began losing half a million dollars each year. Ticket sales declined. The reliance on patrons increased. Donor fatigue set in. The musicians agreed to salary cuts, guest artists lowered fees, the season was shortened, and pieces that required a large orchestra were avoided. In the end, it was all for naught.

The Syracuse Symphony Orchestra's first conductor, Karl Kritz, came to Syracuse in 1961. The Austrian native wanted to make America his home, so he took on the difficult task of starting an orchestra in Syracuse. He initiated a singers-in-residence program and regularly performed concerts and opera. The SSO was not in the best shape when Kritz came. "We had no money, no organization, and no discipline," recalled violinist Carl Silfer, who became concertmaster. But when the Symphony Guild, under the leadership of Carolyn Hopkins, hired conductor Kritz and a business manager, the situation improved dramatically. Kritz adhered to what was called the Viennese, no-nonsense school of conducting. He insisted that all the musicians audition for their seats. He jumped up and down on the podium and threw batons. Nonetheless, he was loved by his musicians. "He was a remarkable man, demanding of his players, and yet after concerts he would go out with us," remembered principal trumpeter George Coble. Kritz combined great baton technique with what principal flutist John Oberbrunner called "sheer willpower and Prussian strength."

Karl Kritz served as a mentor to Calvin Custer, who joined the SSO as a keyboardist and horn and brass performer and was then appointed associate conductor and resident conductor. Custer was also a member of the orchestra's rock and percussion ensembles in which he played numerous instruments, including keyboard and guitar. Custer created and conducted orchestral arrangements of popular music. His stirring arrangement of the national anthem was the rousing send-off of each concert season of the SSO, but his arrangements were also performed by orchestras across the country, including the Boston Pops. The Syracuse Symphony released a CD of Custer's arrangements on the disc *Big Band Bash* in 2006.

In its first season under Karl Kritz's baton, the orchestra performed four subscription concerts in Lincoln Auditorium at Central Tech High School, eight young people's concerts, and one pops concert. By the end of its third season, permanent chamber groups had been formed—a string quartet, a woodwind quintet, a brass quintet, and a percussion ensemble. On December 11, 1969, during a performance of the Sibelius Violin Concerto with renowned soloist Itzhak Perlman, Kritz suffered a heart attack. He rested during intermission and returned to the podium to conduct the American premiere of a symphony by Austrian composer Franz Schmidt. The next day, he was hospitalized. Sadly, he died on December 17. An editorial in the *Syracuse Post Standard* noted that "Kritz had studied under Schmidt in Vienna and he was determined to present his symphony." His obituary read: "Karl Kritz came here when there was nothing. He built for us a symphony orchestra and an opera company. These creations he inspired, along with the personal memories of his tender friendships with so many of us, will sustain Syracuse in the future."

In 1965, the Ford Foundation announced that "in the largest single action in the history of organized philanthropic support of the arts," it was appropriating $85 million for symphony orchestras throughout the United States. It declared: "By placing the nation's rich orchestral resources on a sounder financial footing, the program seeks to insure [sic] continued quality, extend fine music to a greater audience, and attract future generations of musicians by raising the income of orchestra players." At that time, the SSO was the eighth largest metropolitan orchestra in the United States with the twelfth largest budget. The orchestra was tasked with achieving the goals of increased community service, extension of educational services, a longer concert season, and improved musician salary scales. The symphony received the grant in two parts: $250,000 in five annual installments of $50,000 and $750,000 to be held in escrow for 10 years until matched by community support. The Ford Foundation grant allowed the SSO to grow its budget, record and broadcast its concerts, and reach more than 225,000 audience members during its 39-week season.

The local orchestral music radio station, WONO-FM, headed by Henry Fogel, partnered with the SSO to record and broadcast its concerts. Fogel, who went on to become president of the Chicago Symphony and then of the League of American Orchestras, recalls that "the performance level of the Syracuse Symphony Orchestra was without question much higher than one could expect from a city of that size. High-level music-making on an extremely professional level is not something cities the size of Syracuse can hear on a regular basis." Fogel conceived and hosted a radio marathon to benefit the orchestra in 1968, patterning it on the Jerry Lewis Muscular Dystrophy telethon. He raised about $8,000. The format swept the country and became a staple of public radio fundraising that continues to this day. (Photograph by Steffan Aletti.)

Karl Kritz was succeeded in 1971 by Frederik Prausnitz, a German-born American conductor and teacher noted for his commitment to use not widely performed music, such as that of Carl Ruggles, William Walton, Elliott Carter, and Roger Sessions. Prausnitz was the author of *Roger Sessions: How a "Difficult" Composer Got That Way* and a conducting textbook, *Score and Podium*. He had appeared as a guest conductor with the SSO in 1970, conducting a Mahler symphony, and on the strength of that appearance, he was offered the position. But while critics appreciated his contemporary programming, the SSO board was less thrilled with his style and his commitment to the avant-garde. Prausnitz tended to ignore the disgruntlement of board members, but one night he went to the podium during intermission and asked for public backing. The board nonetheless bought out the final year of his contract in 1974 with the following statement: "A great basketball coach can make the players better than they can play . . . and you have just not done that for us."

A Committee for the Protection of Prausnitz and the Syracuse Symphony Orchestra was formed to restore the conductor to his post, but board members argued that their decision was based on a decline in subscriptions and that Prausnitz lacked the popular appeal needed to attract audiences. Jon Newsom, director of the music division at the Library of Congress, noted that Prausnitz's work "gained him great critical acclaim but his uncompromising zeal in presenting new and different music lost him local financial support and his position." Prausnitz had commissioned Roger Sessions's Ninth Symphony, which was dedicated to him, although by the time of its premiere, he had been relieved of his conducting post, and the work was premiered by his successor, Christopher Keene. (Courtesy of the Onondaga Historical Association.)

Christopher Keene came to conduct in Syracuse in 1975 when he was just 28 years old. His first love was opera, and his almost 10 years with the SSO were a symphonic interlude in a conducting career that was so opera-centric that his SSO conducting years are barely mentioned in his Wikipedia biography. But that decade was profoundly impactful for the orchestra and its audiences. Keene's youth, vigor, exuberance, and eloquence made him the most exciting conductor that Syracuse had ever experienced. He bounded on stage for each performance, engaged the audience with explanations and enthusiasm, had to have a rail installed on the podium to keep him from flying off it, and conducted every piece with verve and vivacity and a sensitivity to the individuality of the orchestra's players. He led the orchestra's debut at Carnegie Hall in 1978; he led the SSO there again in 1980 and 1982. He made the orchestra's first recordings: Handel's *Messiah* with the Syracuse University Oratorio Society in Lincoln Auditorium in 1975; Stephen Douglas Burton's Symphony No. 2, *Ariel*, in Syracuse's then new John H. Mulroy Civic Center in 1978; and Keith Jarrett's concerto *The Celestial Hawk* at Carnegie Hall in 1980.

Christopher Keene's impact on the Syracuse musical community was profound. He was, in the words of cellist Gregory Wood, "determined to grow the orchestra"—and he did so with tremendous success, bringing energy and excitement to every performance. The Keene years were notable not only for his drive and enthusiasm but also for the opening in 1976 of the orchestra's first dedicated space: the Crouse Hinds Concert Theater in the John H. Mulroy Civic Center. One of the largest stages in Upstate New York, the theater had 2,000 seats on three tiers with no center orchestra aisle, eight mezzanine boxes, and six balcony boxes. It took 10 years to build at a cost of $24 million. At the orchestra's first concert in the new hall on January 15, 1976, Ella Fitzgerald sang works by Duke Ellington and George Gershwin. Also on the program were two Samuel Barber pieces and a work entitled *What Is There to Sing About?*, commissioned by the Cultural Resources Council and conducted by its composer, Tony Award–winner Charles Strouse.

World premieres of new works were another hallmark of Christopher Keene's tenure. In addition to the aforementioned Ninth Symphony by Roger Sessions, Keene conducted the first performances of Jay Reise's Second Symphony, John Corigliano's *Three Hallucinations for Orchestra*, and Howard Boatwright's Symphony with the SSO. Contemporary composers such as Carlos Chavez, Michael Tippett, and Karel Husa were invited to conduct by Keene, who believed in championing new music. The Syracuse Symphony made the leap from minor to major during Keene's leadership. The category refers solely to budget size, and as the SSO's budget grew, it crossed the threshold to become the smallest of the 30 or so major orchestras in North America. Keene noted that the one critical factor in the orchestra's growth was funding. He pointed out that while the orchestra had improved in the last several years, like many orchestras across the country, money was still the critical issue. The orchestra needed a firm financial foundation to allow it to grow. "It needed financial stability so we could attract outstanding musicians from across the country," he said. (Courtesy of the Library of Congress, Bernard Gotfryd Photograph Collection.)

Guest conductors added luster to the SSO concert schedule and stories to the orchestra's lore. Audiences thrilled when Arthur Fiedler or Leon Fleischer took the podium. When the illustrious conductor Leopold Stokowski (above) came to conduct the Syracuse Symphony in 1971, it was quite an event. Stokowski was 89 years old. Concertmaster Louis Krasner recalled that Stokowski was to conduct Beethoven's Fifth Symphony with its famous opening measures, and the orchestra eagerly awaited instructions as to how he wanted them to play. But Stokowski said nothing. He merely raised his hand and gave the downbeat. The musicians played as they thought he wanted, but the result was not very coordinated. The players waited for Stokowski to direct them, to explain how to play Beethoven. Instead, he raised his hand again and simply said, "Play better." This was repeated again and again, with Stokowski saying only, "Play better," until finally both conductor and musicians were satisfied.

When Christopher Keene left Syracuse to return to his primary love, opera, his place was filled by Kazuyoshi Akiyama, who became music director in 1985. A *New York Times* article with the unfortunate headline "Japanese To Direct Syracuse Symphony" revealed that "Kazuyoshi Akiyama, a conductor of the Tokyo Symphony Orchestra and a former conductor of the American Symphony Orchestra in New York City, will become the principal conductor of the Syracuse Symphony Orchestra in September." In 1974, Akiyama made his debut with the Tokyo Symphony and was soon named the orchestra's music director and permanent conductor. At the age of 44, he became the Syracuse Symphony's fourth conductor in 25 years. Peter Rabinowitz notes that while Akiyama was known "for his precision, his sensitivity, his depth of musical knowledge, and his rapport, . . . he also championed huge works like Strauss's *Alpine Symphony* and Mahler's Second Symphony." Rabinowitz adds, "Few who experienced them will forget the way he handled the room-filling array of percussion in Takemitsu's *From Me Flows What You Call Time* or the antiphonal brass in the Berlioz Requiem."

Kazuyoshi Akiyama was described by local composer and music critic Earl George as "skillful, accomplished and the most musically sensitive of all the SSO's conductors." George, however, felt that while Akiyama's musicians "rightly, worship and respect him," he did not establish "the kind of intimate personal rapport with listeners that swells audiences." Fabio Mechetti, who was hired as Akiyama's assistant conductor, said of him, "Akiyama is one of the greatest musicians I've ever known. I've never encountered anyone with a deeper love for music or a more thorough knowledge of it, or anyone who could convey that love and knowledge to an orchestra better than Akiyama." Akiyama's initial three-year appointment was extended to eight years and then he was named conductor emeritus. His rapport with the orchestra continued even after he left, as noted by a *Post Standard* review: "Whenever conductor emeritus Kazuyoshi Akiyama returns to Syracuse, performances tend to exhibit an extra spark and zing. It's almost like a group of students placed before a onetime teacher, all eager to show that they remember the lessons they have learned."

In 1988, Maestro Akiyama conducted the SSO at Carnegie Hall with guest artist Elmar Oliveira. The *New York Times* said: "Elmar Oliveira and Nathaniel Rosen won the Tchaikovsky competition in Moscow and the Syracuse Symphony Orchestra commissioned a double concerto for the pair, by Ezra Laderman. It was [performed] in convincing fashion when the orchestra visited Carnegie Hall." Finances were a major factor when Akiyama announced in 1993 that he was leaving. He said the orchestra's financial realities prevented him from realizing his artistic visions. His SSO salary was $140,000 per season. He was criticized for his lack of fundraising skill. He responded, "Many prominent conductors command a much greater salary than I, and perhaps these people don't know that I had renegotiated my salary, giving back one-third, in an attempt to help the orchestra financially. Perhaps they also don't know that I, too, have not been paid for last year." He further asserted that he was hired to be a music director, not a fundraiser. Akiyama's successor, associate conductor Fabio Mechetti, was to be paid $85,000 per season.

Fabio Mechetti served as associate conductor of the SSO from 1989 to 1993 before becoming music director in 1993. The Brazilian-born Mechetti was widely noted for conducting many of his first SSO engagements strictly from memory. Music critic David Abrams wrote of Mechetti that the SSO players would say his ear is superb, and he knew precisely what sound he wanted the orchestra to achieve. His "first acquaintance" charisma allowed him to take command of the orchestra immediately at his audition for the associate conductor's position under Kazuyoshi Akiyama. One of five finalists for the job, Mechetti was given just 10 minutes to work with the orchestra. "Mechetti was the only one who made it seem as if it was his orchestra, and he did so immediately," remembers former principal flutist John Oberbrunner.

During his tenure with the orchestra, Fabio Mechetti was respected for his devotion to musical excellence. "I'm in this business to do the best I possibly can as a musician . . . meaning the highest possible artistic level of performance," Mechetti said. According to orchestra members, he arrived at rehearsals utterly prepared and often conducted entire symphonies without a score, saying that "I feel more involvement with the musicians if I am not looking at the score. There's a lot of communication that happens between the conductor and the musicians that you need to be not only listening to what's happening but looking and making visual contact, and if your head is stuck in the score, you lose a lot of that, at least for me, that sort of connection." Mechetti's intense professionalism was a factor that led to his decision to resign from the Syracuse Symphony. "I wanted to see this orchestra becoming bigger and better than it is. I did not find resonance to these wishes of mine in the long term," he said.

Native American Daniel Hege was widely recognized as one of America's finest young conductors, earning critical acclaim for his fresh interpretations of standard repertoire and his commitment to creative programming. A Nez Perce, Hege began making headlines in 1990 when he won a national conducting competition and became music director of the Young Musicians Foundation Debut Orchestra. Hege was named music director of the Syracuse Symphony Orchestra in 1999. He was very well received. Music critic David Abrams wrote, "He led the musicians with precise beats, dependable cues and care and attention to matters of both tempo and dynamics. His is not a theatrical style, and his mannerisms exhibit no pretensions. He just rolls up his sleeves and gets right down to work. Only this work looks like fun." Hege himself said he wanted to "make great music" in Syracuse and "fill the house for every concert." Orchestral music, he declared, is "a civilizing force in our lives. Just about every human being loves music of some kind, and orchestral music is the real rock on which everything else is built."

Highlights of Daniel Hege's leadership included an expanded partnership between the SSO and Syracuse University and the orchestra's first recordings in 25 years. In 2003, Hege led the orchestra in its fifth performance at Carnegie Hall. Under Hege's baton, the orchestra released a classics CD in 2000, a holiday pops CD in 2002, and *Big Band Bash* in 2006. Hege described the important contributions the symphony made to the community, not only in concert but through outreach activities, including two youth orchestras. "These high-level professional musicians provide an enormous resource to our region, not just musically, or just within the SSO, but in the broader sense of culture, through teaching, playing and serving as role models for young people. They provide a wide range of education, entertainment and culture, and they add a great deal to the fabric of our community," he said. Hege's contract was renewed for three years, and had he been able to fulfill the extension, Hege would have held the position longer than any of his predecessors.

Serious issues surrounding the SSO's financial stability had begun to surface in the 1980s. The musicians went on strike several times in the 1980s and 1990s. After a bitter 14-week strike in 1983, music director Christopher Keene stated, "I was horrified by the strike—everybody lost." In 2009, the musicians themselves proposed a wage freeze to help the orchestra through yet another difficult economic period. The players believed that concessions would allow the orchestra to return to financial stability. They were wrong. In 2011, management requested still further cuts from the musicians, stating that things had deteriorated to the point that the orchestra would not be able to make it through its upcoming season. Despite an agreement, disaster struck. The symphony's board of trustees voted to suspend operations. The orchestra's 61 core and 14 contract players were laid off.

The announcement was stark: "The management of the Syracuse Symphony Orchestra has announced the suspension of the remainder of its scheduled performance season due to a budgetary crisis." The SSO, celebrating its 50th anniversary, had more than 20 concerts remaining, including a guest appearance by renowned cellist Yo-Yo Ma. However, a substantial shortfall in revenues had placed the orchestra in a fiscal crisis. An emergency fundraising campaign, begun at the start of the year, raised over $700,000 but failed to overcome the shortfall. Those who had purchased tickets for the Ma concert lost their money, as did those who had contributed to the campaign to save the symphony. (Photograph by Mike Greenlar.)

The impact of the canceled concerts was devastating to the orchestra and the community, but the desire for symphonic music was inextinguishable. As the community gained confidence in the orchestra's ability to operate in a more sustainable way, many funders, including the Syracuse Symphony Foundation, CNY Arts, and Onondaga County stepped up to help build a future for symphonic music in Central New York. Support for the orchestra's musicians was clear on social media. One poster noted that "the musicians of Symphony Syracuse have organized 37 concerts on their own since bankruptcy last year," and another posted, "this is a great testimony of perseverance and a great example to our children and community. Thanks for what you do and believing in it!"

Shortly after the bankruptcy in May 2011, the musicians of the orchestra formed a foundation with a name—Symphony Syracuse. Never intended to be the successor to the SSO, Symphony Syracuse was called a "lifeboat" organization by the musicians. According to Jon Garland, "The musicians decided that 'Syracuse' needed to be in the title, and we liked the play on words."

The ensemble, typically performing with former members of the SSO, played seven full orchestra concerts, including appearances at the state fairgrounds on the Fourth of July, Watertown, Hamilton, Fayetteville, Skaneateles, and Rome. Musicians doubled as staff members, with Jon Garland taking the lead.

Parallel to efforts by Symphony Syracuse, the Syracuse Symphony Foundation, and the Syracuse Philharmonic, a group of arts, cultural, and higher education institutions gathered together for a "Summit on the Symphony." Organized by Hamilton College music faculty member and conductor Heather Buchman, the summit included representatives from Cayuga Community College, Cornell University, Hobart and William Smith Colleges, Ithaca College School of Music, Le Moyne College, Onondaga Community College, State University College at Oswego, Syracuse University, Syracuse Opera, Society for New Music, Syracuse Friends of Chamber Music, the Cultural Resources Council of Syracuse and Onondaga County, the Arts and Culture Leadership Alliance of Central New York, and the Onondaga County executive's office. Former musicians of the SSO also attended the summit.

Symphony Syracuse continued to perform concerts during the winter of 2012. Robert Daino, head of Central New York's public broadcasting station, convened a team of board members to form yet another new organization. Daino had been a board member of the Syracuse Philharmonic and had a deep interest in preserving symphonic music for future generations of Central New Yorkers. After months of planning, recruiting, strategizing, and building consensus, a new organization, Musical Associates of Central New York (MACNY), was announced in September 2012. Jesse Rosen, president of the League of American Orchestras, said that the challenge the organization faced was to "show the community that the organization is one that can be depended upon and that it is inspiring the confidence of key stakeholders in the community to gain some momentum so that others begin to want to participate."

Three

ONWARD, SYMPHORIA!

When the Syracuse Symphony Orchestra Board of Directors voted to cease operations, no refunds were issued for the eagerly anticipated Yo-Yo Ma concert or the rest of the season. Those who had donated to the "Keep the Music Playing" campaign had not been thanked. The musicians decided to play a concert for all of the patrons who had supported the orchestra. That performance, along with two benefit performances organized with help from Hamilton College, set into motion a series of over 40 performances by Symphony Syracuse that eventually led to the formation of Symphoria.

The orchestra members formed an unincorporated foundation, the Musical Associates of Central New York, to secure insurance, accept donations, and temporarily present performances. Musicians from the orchestra took on roles in personnel management, fundraising, operations, library, marketing, and stage management. Summer concert presenters were contacted and assured that, while the SSO was gone, the musicians were not. Because the SSO's assets were tied up in the bankruptcy, there was a scramble to get chairs, stands, and music for each performance. Somehow, eight full orchestral concerts and several ensemble performances were produced that summer. Forty performances were presented during the 2011–2012 concert season. The orchestra performed masterworks concerts featuring violinist Elmar Oliveira, cellist Julie Albers, and conductors Stuart Robertson and Fabio Mechetti.

Behind the scenes, dozens of meetings were taking place to form a permanent organization. A business plan was crafted to secure financial support. In the fall of 2012, a smooth transition took place between the musicians' foundation and a new organization that had secured support from major funders. All former SSO musicians who remained in the area became core members of a new orchestra. Its name was announced at a sold-out performance in December, and a subscription series was announced for the spring concert season.

The musicians and board of Symphoria viewed the orchestra as an integral part of the economic, social, and cultural life of Syracuse, and they are proud of what they have accomplished in their first decade. They believe that their unique model of music making will allow them to live up to their motto: "Onward, Symphoria!"

Symphoria's board members included former SSO musicians, community members, and participants in the Summit on the Symphony. Symphoria anticipated a budget of $1.5 to $2 million under a cooperative arrangement with a core group of players who would receive compensation only after all other expenses were paid. The musicians were paid less than $10,000 each. They waived union pay scale. There were 52 core musicians, an administrative staff of six, and a production crew of two. Only three people had full-time jobs. The musicians had access to health care but no retirement fund. The back office operation was strictly bare bones.

Jon Garland had served as chair of the musicians committee for the Syracuse Symphony Orchestra and was one of Symphoria's founding members. A member of the Symphoria horn section and an instructor of horn performance at Syracuse University's Setnor School of Music, Garland believed that a cooperative governance model allowed Symphoria to be more collaborative and open than a traditionally structured orchestra. "Musicians are very involved in the governance of the organization and artistic decisions," he noted. Garland served as managing director when Symphoria was founded. Since then, when not playing or teaching, he can be found in the Symphoria office serving as operations manager.

The orchestra kept on concertizing. It undertook a collaboration with Syracuse Opera for a performance of *Tosca*, performed with choral groups from Syracuse University, and presented two concerts in association with the Syracuse International Film Festival. Other community collaborations were held, such as *Kaddish*, a community-wide Holocaust commemoration with the Jewish Federation of Central New York, InterFaith Works, and the Syracuse University Oratorio Society in a program of "music of remembrance and hope."

Symphoria began its first full season with the theme "Overture to the Future." It named Sean O'Loughlin as principal pops conductor. O'Loughlin had grown up in Lyncourt and studied music at Syracuse University. Of his appointment, O'Loughlin said, "I am so proud to serve as principal pops conductor of Symphoria. It's a top-level ensemble." O'Loughlin had worked with Symphoria since its inception. A composer and arranger whose music was characterized by vibrant rhythms, passionate melodies, and colorful scoring, he had had commissions from the Boston Pops Orchestra, the Los Angeles Philharmonic, and the Hollywood Bowl Orchestra and had conducted many orchestras, including the Boston Pops, the San Francisco Symphony, and the Chicago Symphony. As a native Syracusan, O'Loughlin said that he was "humbled and thrilled to be continuing this journey with Symphoria," adding that, "From the musicians to the staff to the audience, this is an incredible environment in which to make music. I consider it a privilege to be part of the growth of this orchestra across the region. We have so much in store for the coming years."

To help Symphoria get established, several well-known musicians came to conduct or perform with the orchestra. The guest appearance of JoAnn Falletta, music director of the Buffalo Philharmonic, had a special significance. Falletta had been a guest conductor for the Syracuse Symphony as it was expiring. In selecting the pieces for her first concert with Symphoria, she said she "wanted to do something that would feature the musicians, especially the Rimsky piece, which is filled with sorrows and difficult virtuoso playing from the whole symphony. . . . I thought that was a great way to celebrate this extraordinary group of musicians." The program, a travelogue through the Near East, showcased Nielsen's *Aladdin Suite*, Ravel's *Shéhérazade*, and Rimsky-Korsakov's *Scheherazade*. A local reviewer reported that "when the stormy final movement ended, the audience took up the tumult with a full five minutes of cheering, stomping and whistling. During the standing ovation, Falletta repeatedly swept her arms toward the soloists and reflected the applause from herself to the orchestra, giving full credit for an outstanding performance to the Symphoria musicians."

Musical Associates of Central New York began presenting concerts in October 2012 and in December announced the new orchestra's name—Symphoria, chosen to reflect "the feeling of euphoria one gets after hearing an amazing piece of orchestral music, whether string or wind ensemble, full orchestra or otherwise." "Music in the key of CNY" was chosen as its tagline, and "Onward, Symphoria!" became its motto. Sean O'Loughlin premiered his eponymous piece, *Symphoria*, as a concert opener. Robert Daino told the audience that forming the new orchestra involved "breaking down barriers, building up trust and bringing people together and applying a no-rules approach that centered on the future." He said, "We looked to the past only to learn from its strength and avoid potential pitfalls. The one principle we lived by was that failure was not an option. Our debut tonight is proof of that."

Symphoria needed a music director, but it was a challenge to fund the position. The musicians had cut most management positions and $4 million from the budget. They had also cut their own base salaries, from $30,000 to $10,000. Lawrence Loh, music director of the Northeastern Pennsylvania Philharmonic in nearby Scranton, had called Syracuse whenever he needed a sub to fill a spot in his orchestra. "We knew there were a lot of good musicians there not working at the time and we were happy to support them and have them come play with us," Loh said. Perhaps it was only natural that when Syracuse needed a conductor, it would consider Loh. When Loh was asked to come conduct Symphoria as a guest conductor in 2012, he did not know he was in the running for a permanent position. He was established in Pittsburgh, where he was the resident conductor of the Pittsburgh Symphony Orchestra.

When Lawrence Loh came to Symphoria as a guest conductor for the second time, board members and musicians unanimously agreed that he was the person they wanted at the helm. Loh was equally enthusiastic. "The musicians have a very obvious personal stake in the organization's success. And so do I," he said. "We are all responsible for Symphoria. Every one of us." In his first concert as music director, Loh led the musicians in Beethoven's famous Fifth Symphony. Loh declared that he wanted to establish the orchestra more firmly in the community and gain its trust.

Reaction to Lawrence Loh's appointment was extremely positive. Jon Garland, Symphoria musician and board member, said that "Loh is the perfect fit. We're really thrilled to have him." Linda Hartsock, director of Syracuse's civic engagement initiative Connective Corridor, said that bringing on Loh was a "bold move," adding, "I think it'll be exciting not just for Symphoria, but for Syracuse. The word that's used most often to describe him is 'electrifying.' " For Loh, taking the position was a leap of faith. He wanted to meet Symphoria patrons, donors, and its community. "The job extends so far beyond the podium," he noted. "I think of myself as a communicator, both in rehearsals with the musicians, verbally and nonverbally, and with the audience, to build a bridge between the stage and the audience." Loh was appointed music director in 2014 and began in 2015.

Under Loh's direction, the orchestra continued to increase its partnerships with other organizations. "We all coexist, and we all have the same mission: trying to work to enrich lives through great art," he said, announcing that he would be exploring new ways to unite Symphoria with the public. He planned to travel with the musicians to different venues around the city to perform different kinds of concerts. Between the masterworks, pops, casual, and kids concert series, Loh hoped to provide music to as many listeners as possible. His opening concert, *Symphonie Fantastique*, featured pianists Christina (left) and Michelle Naughton (right) performing Poulenc's Concerto for Two Pianos and Orchestra. Loh's first-season highlights included an evening with cellist Julie Albers, an afternoon with violinist Itzhak Perlman for Beethoven's Violin Concerto, pianist Orion Weiss performing Gershwin's *Rhapsody in Blue*, a pops night with music from Disney movies, Brahms's *German Requiem*, a Shostakovich symphony, and works by Ravel and Saint-Saëns. He also began to introduce new composers, artists, and music and new formats to Symphoria's repertoire.

Symphoria paid a musical tribute to Shakespeare on the 400th anniversary of his death in 2016. Scenes from *Romeo and Juliet* were performed by acting students from Syracuse University as Maestro Loh led the orchestra in musical pieces that illuminated the bard's brilliance. "Composers have always found the writing of William Shakespeare particularly inspiring," Loh explained. "So, we have a rich variety of musical reflections on his works. In programming this concert, Symphoria musicians looked to ballet, incidental music and musical theater. The presentation of scenes from 'Romeo and Juliet,' bring Prokofiev's inspiring music even closer to Shakespeare's brilliant text."

Pamela Murchison was named executive director of Symphoria in 2019. She had been vice president of development with the West Virginia Symphony Orchestra, where she played flute and piccolo. Murchison attended a Symphoria concert prior to accepting the position. She said, "I was greatly impressed with the level of performance and with the audience's positive response to that concert. Symphoria has all elements necessary for success already in place: a strong board of directors, a talented and disciplined group of musicians, carefully curated seasons, and a supportive community. I'm looking forward to becoming part of all this."

Symphoria staff responded vigorously when a *New York Times* article about upstate orchestras failed to mention it, declaring, "Symphoria emerged from the ashes of the old institution much as new growth emerges in the wake of a forest fire—green and vibrant and bursting with life. And we are growing audiences, engaging community members, and building our base of support as part of a widespread revitalization of this beautiful and historic community. Our core of 50 professional musicians have chosen to take the risk of the new symphony on themselves—if we succeed, they succeed."

Four of Symphoria's musicians do double duty as staff members. Current musicians serving as staff members are flutist Kelly Covert (right), Symphoria's development associate; violist Arvilla Wendland (left), personnel manager; bassist Spencer Phillips (below), the orchestra's librarian; and horn player Jon Garland, operations director. Symphoria moved to new offices at 450 Salina Street in the spring of 2022.

Symphoria created a values statement in which it expressed its aspiration to the "quality of being outstanding" and noted that "we present the highest quality performances of a wide variety of symphonic and chamber music in diverse styles, maintaining a balance between our stewardship of the great symphonic tradition of the past while also presenting under-represented voices from the past and present and the best new music written for orchestra. Symphoria brings world-renowned guest artists to our area, to collaborate with our fabulous musicians who are residents of the CNY community." Symphoria brought outstanding musical artists to the community, such as Garrick Ohlsson, Zuill Bailey, Julian Schwarz, and pianists Natasha Paremski (above) and Jon Nakamatsu. In what was described as "an act of daring most pianists would never even consider," Paremski performed all four of Rachmaninoff's technically challenging piano concertos in two back-to-back nights in a tour de force program on one weekend.

Internationally celebrated pianist Jon Nakamatsu returned to Symphoria to play Ravel's Concerto in G Major for Piano and Orchestra. The evening's opener was Ballade in A Minor by the Black composer Samuel Coleridge-Taylor. The final piece was a Rachmaninoff symphony. Program notes by Peter Rabinowitz for the evening contrasted the careers of the three composers, born less than three years apart. In 1898, "Rachmaninoff was reeling from the failure of his First Symphony, a failure so complete that he abandoned composing for years. Ravel was about to be kicked out of his composition class at the Conservatoire for failing fugue exams twice. Coleridge-Taylor, in contrast, was on an upward trajectory. Edward Elgar had been asked to write a piece for a prestigious festival but since he was over-committed, he recommended that the commission be directed to Coleridge-Taylor." The resulting Ballade was a tremendous success, and Coleridge-Taylor should have taken a place in the constellation of major composers. Alas, as Rabinowitz wrote, "We don't know what trajectory Coleridge-Taylor would have followed if he had not died of pneumonia brought on by overwork."

Symphoria's board of directors extended the contracts of music director Loh and principal pops conductor O'Loughlin. Board chair Mary Ann Tyszko said Loh and O'Loughlin had become an integral part of Symphoria and that they, along with the professional musicians, created a positive experience for audiences every time they performed. Said Loh, "Since the first time I stepped on the podium here, I have felt a true connection to our musicians and the Central New York audience. I am beyond thrilled to sign an extension to continue with Symphoria, which has always been an innovative orchestra, and the pandemic has shown the resilience of our musicians. At a time when many orchestras stopped performing, we adapted, persevered and even thrived. I look forward to continuing the progress we've made." Sean O'Loughlin added, "I am humbled and thrilled to be continuing the journey with Symphoria. From the musicians to the staff to the audience, it is an incredible place to make music. We have so much in store for the coming years. Onward!"

In 2021, Symphoria finalized a mission and vision statement. It proclaimed the orchestra's mission "to engage and inspire all community members throughout Central New York with outstanding orchestral and ensemble performances, and innovative education and outreach initiatives." That mission was aligned to a vision "to contribute to a diverse, vibrant, equitable, and culturally rich community through the power of great music, and in so doing, enhance the quality of life and economic vitality of Central New York." The orchestra also delineated three values that would define its work: innovation, excellence, and collaboration. It declared that by using creativity and optimism and being flexible and visionary, it would adapt to "an ever-changing world." Notably, Symphoria wanted to "find fun for everyone" because "what is the point of being innovative without having fun?" The Spark series concerts were designed to expand the orchestra's approach to programming and to reach new audiences in new and innovative ways.

Creativity was much in evidence in an inspired junction of music and writing when famed children's author Bruce Coville added a haunting voice to *It Was a Dark and Stormy Night*, Symphoria's Halloween concert in 2014. Winners of the annual Bruce Coville Halloween story writing contest attended the performance. Darth Vader was on the podium, conducting a pharaoh, an escaped prisoner, Dorothy, a 10-foot-high clarinet, and a handful of Tootsie Rolls in the second violin section. Coville narrated an original story in a scarlet-lined black cape. Children in full Halloween regalia enjoyed the concert tremendously.

Symphoria's *Music of Space* concert, inspired by the comet ISON and presented at the Museum of Science & Technology, was one of the orchestra's Spark series concerts, designed to get the orchestra out into the community so that people could interface with it in settings that reflected the concert's theme. ISON was a sun-grazing comet. Shortly after its discovery, the media reported that it might become brighter than the full moon. However, as events transpired, it never became bright enough to be readily visible to the naked eye. Furthermore, it broke apart as it passed close to the sun. In a recap of the comet's story, the full orchestra played several pieces and then broke into solo and ensemble groupings scattered around the museum. Concertgoers enjoyed appetizers and refreshments while listening to mini performances before returning to the main hall for the reassembled orchestra's performance of Gustav Holst's "Neptune, the Mystic" from *The Planets*.

Another out-of-the-box Symphoria collaboration and performance was the *Video Games Live* show at the Landmark Theater. "We are anything but a traditional orchestral music show," said Tommy Tallarico, host of the multimedia concert at which full-length versions or medleys of music from video games such as *Halo, Zelda, Final Fantasy*, and *Kingdom Hearts* were performed. A video game played on the main screen while two side screens showed close-ups of the musicians. A few concertgoers were selected to play games on stage while the musicians kept up with the action. "Video Games Live was an opportunity to introduce a new generation of young people to the Symphony," according to Tallarico. "It's the new orchestral music of the 21st century," he said. Symphoria and the Landmark Theater partnered to present *Video Games Live* to coincide with the Art of the Video Game exhibition at the Everson Museum of Art.

Pops conductor Sean O'Loughlin was sure that doo-wop, a genre of rhythm and blues music that originated in the Black community in the 1940s, would be a hit in Syracuse. "They've come up with such a cool concept by taking the tradition of doo-wop singing and applying it to generations of pop music," he explained. Five singers reimagined popular music from the mid-20th century to the 21st. By transforming the original style of contemporary music, they allowed the audience to hear their interpretations of what contemporary artists would sound like when heard through the filter of doo-wop.

A highlight of the 2017 season was the guest appearance of violinist Anne Akiko Meyers, a performer known for her pure sound, passion-filled performances, and poetic interpretations. The top-selling orchestral instrumentalist performed award-winning composer Mason Bates's violin concerto, which was commissioned and written for her in 2012. Bates is one of the most-performed living composers in the United States. Meyers had risen to fame in her early childhood, playing at the Emmys and with major orchestras by the age of 12. She has more than 30 albums, two of which debuted at No. 1 on the Billboard charts. Meyers, who was very well received at her first appearance with the orchestra, said she was looking forward to performing again in Central New York and to collaborating with the musicians of Symphoria.

Working in partnership with other arts organizations was key to Symphoria's rebirth, providing an important way to create a larger impact by involving more people and pooling the best of talent and skills. Symphoria took pride in working with local organizations and artists to give them additional forums through which to showcase their work. The Syracuse University Oratorio Society, a mixed vocal ensemble comprised of Syracuse University students and community members directed by John Warren, joined with the symphony's musicians to produce stirring performances of such works as Carl Orff's *Carmina Burana*, Beethoven's Ninth Symphony, Downing's *Credo*, and Verdi's Requiem. The talented singers of the Syracuse Pops Chorus, led by Lou Lemos, regularly join Symphoria for holiday pops and summer concerts.

A unique melding of community music makers occurred when Symphoria performed side by side with the Salt City New Horizons Orchestra, a community orchestra "for those wishing to continue playing after life interrupts and puts skills learned in school on hold," which features players of violin, viola, cello, and bass. Symphoria also partnered with the Onondaga Civic Symphony, comprised of diverse and passionate amateur and professional musicians from all across the Syracuse area, which provides its members with the opportunity to perform symphonic music. Selections included works from John Williams, Bernstein, Tchaikovsky, and others. Joining with other local passionate music lovers and musicians strengthened Symphoria's ties to the community, as Jon Garland acknowledged when he said, "The orchestras that are in the area have been around for many years, so they have a legacy of how they've interacted with the community. But we have a different opportunity because we get to build those relationships."

Symphoria took up the challenge "to educate and influence our surrounding communities with the power of music." One example of its dedication to connecting to the community and its history was the *Achievements of Women in Music* concert, which celebrated Central New York's women who took leadership roles to gain the right to vote. Symphoria featured the work of award-winning women composers in a concert in Oswego that evoked themes of freedom, liberty, and women as changemakers. Symphoria performed Caroline Shaw's *Entre'Acte*, Jennifer Higdon's Concerto for Soprano Sax, Amy Beach's Symphony in E Minor, Missy Mazzoli's *Holy Roller*, and Joan Tower's *Made in America*. Another example was the *Ellis Island: The Dream of America* concert. Music director Lawrence Loh conducted Peter Boyer's 2001 multimedia production that combined dramatic readings, historic film, and orchestral music. The large concert work showcased Symphoria's professional musicians alongside student actors from Syracuse University's Department of Drama who performed texts from the Ellis Island Oral History Project telling specific immigration stories. (Photograph by Brenna Merritt.)

Symphoria sought to create opportunities for growth and diversity in a safe space where all felt welcome, especially musicians and other artists from underrepresented groups, by removing barriers for them to work in the orchestral space. A unique collaboration was formed at *Poe Halloween*, an adults-only concert described as "the perfect ghoulish evening for any Halloween lover." Haitian-born communicator, orator, and performer Ruthnie Angrand recited Edgar Allan Poe's "The Raven" and other poems. The orchestra played Humperdinck's "Witch's Ride" and Saint-Saëns's *Danse Macabre*, and attendees were cautioned: "Try not to have any nightmares once you leave!"

In a concert that could only be called "delectable," Symphoria presented *Symphony of Desserts* under the baton of guest conductor Herbert Smith, a jazz and orchestral musician, teacher, composer, and conductor. *Symphony of Desserts* was a prelude to Valentine's Day. It sweetened the evening with desserts from a popular local business, Rai's Dough Bakeshop and Café. Chef Rai, born into a family of Southern cooks, introduced a lot of interesting ingredients from the Rai's Dough Desserts Bar, including such unusual items as a deconstructed Snickers bar, known to put customers into a candy coma. Chocolate mousse with chocolate ganache, three layers of chocolate cake, and a center of creamy caramel and chopped nuts was also a favorite. Appropriate accompanying orchestral selections included Mascagni's Intermezzo from *Cavalleria Rusticana*, Tchaikovsky's *Romeo and Juliet–Fantasy Overture*, and selections from *My Fair Lady* and the movie *Titanic*.

Stories of the Six Nations was a musical collaboration between Symphoria and the Oneida Nation, presented as both a Spark series concert and a children's concert. Central to each performance was a reading of an updated version of a traditional legend, "Tale of Two Teams," part of a series created by the Oneida Indian Nation Language Program to help teach and preserve the language of the Oneidas. Chelsea Jocko, Oneida Nation Wolf Clan member and language program trainee, narrated the story as Symphoria played background music by Sibelius, Bartok, and Ravel. Images of the pages were projected on a screen so viewers could see the vocabulary words and phonics that were woven into the text, allowing them to acquire language while following the narrative of the story. "The people of the Oneida Nation have made it a priority to preserve their language," said Heather Buchman, who conducted both concerts. A special tribute to honor the memory of Grammy Award winner and internationally renowned singer/composer Joanne Shenandoah was presented by her daughter Leah Shenandoah, a member of the Wolf Clan of the Oneida.

The triumph of the arts over strife, war, apartheid, and genocide was made clear with Symphoria's program *The Promise of Hope*. Guest conductor Michael Lankester quoted John F. Kennedy: "We, too, will be remembered not for victories or defeats in battle or in politics, but for our contributions to the human spirit." The program featured composer Daniel Strong Godfrey's *Towards the Sun*, commissioned by Symphoria for its world premiere at this concert. The works pays tribute to South Africa's first Black president, Nelson Mandela. Percussionists were spotlighted as Godfrey's score was filled with rhythms of the Transkei region, Mandela's home. Godfrey told the audience he had used four sources for the African-like melodies: native freedom songs, village green dances, popular music, and evangelical hymns of the region. Van Robinson and Patricia Albright illuminated the score with quotations from Mandela's works, concluding with his exhortation, "Let us join hands and march into the future together."

The houses were full when the orchestra performed with dance ensembles from local companies, including The Ballet and Dance Center, Empire Center of Dance, and Dance Centre North. The holiday performances became a treasured community tradition for artists and families alike. The opportunity to perform with a full orchestra was a special gift to the young dancers. As one studio put it, "The true purpose of arts education is not necessarily to create more professional dancers or artists. It is to create more complete human beings who are critical thinkers, have curious minds, who can lead productive lives."

Symphoria joined forces with young dancers from the community for whirlwinds of movement, color, and sound at many concerts. Dancing in front of a full orchestra is a unique experience. Most dance recitals are accompanied by a pit orchestra of perhaps one or two dozen instrumentalists. Having a full orchestra producing a wall of sound behind the dancers is another level of artistry. Choreography has to account for the length of the stage rather than its depth, and dance takes place from side to side, never getting too close to the instruments or the edge of the stage.

The Nutcracker is a traditional symphonic holiday presentation, but Symphoria and CirqOvation presented *Nutcracker Twist: An Enchanted Journey* in a completely nontraditional way. A new take on the traditional Christmas fare involved aerialists, jugglers, acrobats, comedians, and other amazing performers who brought Tchaikovsky's classic ballet to life in a spectacular fashion. Dr. Juhanna Rogers, vice president of racial equity and social impact for CenterState CEO's Racial Equity and Social Impact portfolio, narrated the classic Nutcracker story, rewritten with some new variations by Linda Lowen. The performance also included special appearances by Circus Culture of Ithaca and Salt City Burlesque.

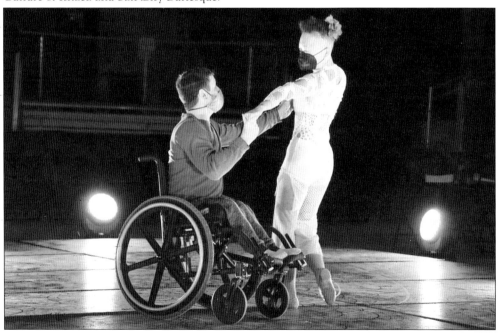

Mindful of its commitment to "find fun for everyone," Symphoria took holiday pops concerts seriously. Because children could attend for free, the concerts became a family tradition for many. Performances featured holiday favorites and soon-to-be favorites and a "cast of thousands," including the Syracuse Pops Chorus, dancers from local troupes and studios, and special guest vocalists, who were sometimes Broadway stars. The whole family could enjoy a spectacular show at minimal cost, saving money for gifts and feasting. The concerts were so appealing that Santa Claus himself was known to drop in and Mrs. Claus sometimes came along for the fun.

Famous guest conductors have always been highlights of symphony concerts, and their appearances generated audience enthusiasm and sometimes stories that became part of the orchestra's lore. When Arthur Fiedler, the legendary Boston Pops conductor, came to Syracuse in 1972, he kept a sponge pad on his music stand. He would press his finger on the sponge, lick it, and turn the page of his score. Only later did the musicians learn that the sponge was soaked with gin. Symphoria took the term "guest conductor" in a different direction with unexpected conductors like Spider Man or Obi Wan Kenobi dropping by to lead the music making.

It was sometimes hard to tell who was having more fun dressing up—the orchestra or the audience. Orchestra musicians abandoned the tails and cummerbunds of old, and the days of formal gowns and tuxedos are long gone. Symphoria welcomed audiences to experience the music attired as they pleased, whether to accommodate the Syracuse winter weather or dressed up for a date night out. The important thing is to enjoy the music—and sometimes that might even mean wearing a costume.

Costumes are part of what makes Symphoria's Halloween concerts fan favorites, not only for the music but for the spirit of frivolity that prevails. The whole orchestra gets into the act, as they demonstrate to the community that orchestral music can be just as much fun as rock or pop. With audience members in costume and some very unusual musicians in the seats, Symphoria proved that orchestral music performances can be very entertaining.

At the heart of all that Symphoria does is the value of collaboration, which it defines as the action of working with someone to produce or create something. Symphoria believes that "we are stronger as a team than we are as individuals" and pledged to "work together in kindness, integrity, and commitment in all interactions, from rehearsals to meetings, to build a better orchestra and a more optimistic community." Music equaled connection in Symphoria's view, and the orchestra strove to assure that its collaborations with partners in the community were "deliberate and intentional as to be meaningful for all participants." It worked to ensure that programs were "created in partnership with the community to connect regional events and history that are relevant to diverse audiences and bring awareness to and celebrate achievements, traditions, and culture of various groups in our community."

Symphoria's structure was well ahead of the curve in terms of organization. Edward Arian, author of *Bach, Beethoven, and Bureaucracy*, a study of organizational dynamics in the orchestra world, emphasized the need for flexibility and the multifaceted nature of musician involvement in the 21st century. "The present demographic revolution projects a multicultural population that will require adaptation by symphony orchestras in terms of new programs and formats to increase community support. The key to change is meaningful participation by musicians in all important decisions. In organizational theory and research, it has been demonstrated that this policy, which confers dignity and respect, leads to a greater employee sense of responsibility for the fate of the institution," he wrote. Symphoria hit the mark in subscribing to the tenet that "every voice in the Symphoria family contributes to our growth and sustainability. We are grateful for a structure that allows musicians, board, and staff connected through music and common goals that serve Symphoria and the community. We allocate time and resources to achieve diverse, equitable, and inclusive representation from the community to Symphoria. We are transparent, candid, and open in our communications."

Since its earliest days, the people of Syracuse placed great emphasis on encouraging young people to experience orchestral music. Symphoria made outreach to young people a priority. The instrument petting zoo and kid-friendly performances are a hallmark of its programming. Designed specifically with families in mind, hour-long performances were held at Inspiration Hall with an interactive pre-concert component. Children could embark on a "symphonic safari" to get to know the orchestra and the instruments in a hands-on experience. Admission was free for children under 18, not only for the children's concerts but for all regular season performances.

In another creative musical initiative, Symphoria partnered with the Connective Corridor, the Everson Museum of Art, the Syracuse University Setnor School of Music, the City of Syracuse, and Onondaga County to distinguish downtown Syracuse as a uniquely creative and collaborative environment and a fun place to live, work, and visit. Family-friendly cajon drums, tembos, babel drums, bell lyres, and papilio bells, all designed for year-round music making, were placed in three public spaces, called Syracuse Sound Stops, and young and old were invited to play, no prior training or musical knowledge required. (Above, courtesy of Percussion Play.)

Children's concerts were always a priority, but of even more significance were young people's orchestras. The Symphoria Youth Orchestra (SYO) allowed students to develop their skills, refine their musicianship, and cultivate an overall appreciation for excellence in music with similarly interested students. Three ensembles were provided for young musicians. The Symphoria Young Artists Orchestra (SYAO) offered an orchestral experience with the most challenging repertoire, somewhat longer rehearsals, and three performance experiences. Sectional coaching was offered by Symphoria musicians for each concert cycle as well as master class opportunities throughout the year. In addition, student musicians joined their professional counterparts to perform on a Symphoria masterworks performance.

The Symphoria Youth Repertory Orchestra (SYRO) offered a full orchestra experience with three performances, including a side-by-side performance with Symphoria. SYRO musicians were even allowed to participate in master class opportunities with visiting guest artists. The SYRO was open to students up to the age of 18. The Symphoria Youth String Orchestra (SYSO) brought together the most talented young string musicians in Central New York to perform a wide variety of string repertoire. The Symphoria Chamber Music program allowed students of all ages to participate in an immersive musical program that explored standard chamber music literature.

Conductor Charles Hazelwood wrote: "The beauty of an orchestra is that there is no clarinet, trumpet, or cello player who is more important than the rest. They all have equal importance and an absolute determination to make everyone else in the room look (and sound) good." The unity that an orchestra inspires is an important life lesson for young people. Paul McShee, youth orchestra music director, believes passionately in the importance of music in the community. He is a champion of new music and the works of underrepresented composers. Becky Dodd, a well-respected teacher of music in the Liverpool Central School District, is the youth strings conductor.

One young violinist explained that what she liked about the youth orchestra "is the challenge and the camaraderie of the group. At my school we have an orchestra but it isn't anywhere close to the talent of SYO musicians. This group gives me an opportunity to express my musicality and learn from my talented peers around me." Research has shown that participation in youth orchestras offers young people the opportunity to develop social networks and skills such as creativity, collaboration, communication, and critical thinking. Being with peers who share a passion for making music can also lead to lifelong friendships and connections.

Playing an instrument is often considered a form of individual expression, distinct from playing on a sports team. But while it definitely is that, playing an instrument in an ensemble is also a powerful way to learn teamwork. In each of Symphoria's three instrumental groups, young musicians work together to form a community based on teamwork and collaboration. Playing together, students listen to one another to better gage and adjust volume, dynamics, and rhythm. Working as one, they create relationships and friendships and become a support system for one another through their common love of music. Intergenerational friendships are another invaluable benefit.

Admission to the SYO program was contingent on a successful audition before a panel of Symphoria musicians. Auditions lasted seven minutes, during which prospective members presented a three- to four-minute solo piece that showcased their playing at its best. Students were welcome to present their current New York State School Music Association (NYSSMA) solo piece or any repertoire that best represented their musicianship. Alternatively, they could prepare contrasting excerpts to show the panel different styles (fast/technical vs. lyrical, for example). The panel also asked for two major scales. One was selected by the student, and the second was chosen by the panel based on the student's level. SYSO required at least one octave, SYRO required at least two octaves, and SYAO required at least three octaves. Auditioners were not eliminated from consideration for a group if they could not play the right number of octaves. One or two octaves played with great sound and intonation was considered better than three that were out of tune and rushed.

Symphoria also encouraged local high school and middle school orchestras and music ensembles to perform on the main stage of the John H. Mulroy Civic Center before Symphoria concerts. It was quite a leap from a high school auditorium to the stage of a 2,000-seat theater, and the descriptor "awesome" was frequently heard. The young musicians and their families were then invited to attend the Symphoria performances (no charge for those under 18) to further inspire them in their love of orchestral music.

One of the most outstanding features of the youth symphony programs were side-by-side concerts at which the young instrumentalists performed with their adult counterparts. It was an exciting and memorable experience for young musicians to sit alongside professionals and perform together. Although students learned from Symphoria musicians through master classes or by attending

regular Symphoria performances, and while many players were also their private teachers, there was nothing as meaningful or thrilling as sitting next to one's mentor and teacher and performing a musical masterpiece together.

The members of the youth ensembles of Symphoria were a dedicated group of young people. When COVID hit, the resiliency of the Symphoria Youth Orchestra members was quite remarkable. Even when the teens had to endure a drastic shift to virtual classrooms, the absence of extracurricular activities, and the lack of socially interaction, they persevered with their music. Symphoria was able to offer a safe, in-person musical experience for all of its youth orchestra members. The Symphoria Youth Orchestra's virtual concerts at Inspiration Hall continued to give students an opportunity to perform during very challenging times.

Symphoria is, in a sense, the community's orchestra, even though it is much more than a community orchestra. Joining with community groups, Symphoria not only raised the level of the musical experience but also engendered goodwill and helped to celebrate special occasions, particularly holidays. Community spirit was added to the holiday spirit as, in addition to Symphoria performances with church choirs, local caroling groups serenaded Symphoria audiences as they arrived for holiday concerts at the John H. Mulroy Civic Center.

No celebration of Christmas would be complete without a stirring performance of George Frideric Handel's oratorio *Messiah*, and no venue was more appropriate for that performance than Syracuse's Cathedral of the Immaculate Conception, where Symphoria joined with the Syracuse Oratorio Society and guest artists for a beautiful rendition of this magnificent music in an entirely suitable setting. Symphoria and the Syracuse Pops Chorus also joined forces to present the Christmas portion of *Messiah*, including the beloved "Hallelujah" chorus, in Oswego.

Collaborations with community organizations create tremendous goodwill. Itzhak Perlman's appearance with Symphoria was sponsored by Temple Concord through its Regina F. Goldenberg Cultural Fund, but the entire community benefitted from having an artist of Perlman's stature come to Central New York. Perlman, who has a long history of performing in Syracuse, was received with reverence and joy. A reviewer wrote, "A collective intake of breath held the audience in absolute silence as the notes from Perlman's instrument climbed to celestial peaks, where he held them at the precipice until they tumbled in a plunging cascade, and people finally exhaled."

When Russia invaded Ukraine in 2022, the Symphoria community wanted to do something to help the millions of refugees who fled the war. Choirs from Syracuse's Ukrainian community churches and the ODESA Ukrainian Dance Ensemble of Syracuse joined Symphoria on stage in a program celebrating music by Ukrainian composers, including Mykola Lysenko's 2002 "Prayer for Ukraine." Ukrainian American conductor Taras Krysa led the orchestra. Krysa was a friend of Lawrence Loh, who was delighted that Central New Yorkers could experience his friend's "immense talent." Tickets to the concert were free, but donations for refugee relief were accepted by InterFaith Works, which handles local refugee resettlement.

The benefit concert for Ukraine was sponsored by Northwestern Mutual of Syracuse, whose managing director, Paul Dodd, said that the plight of Ukraine inspired him to support the Symphoria benefit. Each season, many supporters chose to make the community stronger through their support of Symphoria's work, including the Syracuse Symphony Foundation, CNY Arts, Onondaga County, and the New York State Council on the Arts. Progressive Expert Consulting (PEC) and the Feng family, the Slutzker Family Foundation, and the Allyn Foundation provided title support for concert series. These donors were joined by organizations like the Fred L. Emerson Foundation, the Central New York Community Foundation, Syracuse Sounds of Music Association, the Gifford Foundation, and many other local businesses and foundations. "It would be impossible to recognize the many wonderful friends who bring music to life in Central New York," said executive director Pamela Murchison. "However, every member of the Symphoria family knows that the orchestra's work is only possible because of the incredible generosity of the many lovers of symphonic music in our community."

The COVID-19 pandemic had a devastating impact on musical artists and performing arts organizations. During the pandemic, nearly one-third of major orchestras stopped performing, offering neither live or streamed performances. Over half of smaller-budget orchestras ceased playing. Even when they returned to in-person performance, most orchestras found halls to be filled on average to only 42 percent of capacity. COVID forced the cancellation of two Symphoria concerts of Brahms choral works that would have been collaborations with the Syracuse University Oratorio Society. Three months of concerts had to be cancelled. But then Symphoria encased its musicians in plexiglass booths, masked them, and began to livestream concerts. Music director Lawrence Loh presented pre-concert talks for ticket holders, who signed onto Vimeo accounts one hour prior to performances. Concerts were livestreamed from Inspiration Hall, where musicians were physically distanced and protected by the heavy shields. Several orchestra members pivoted to individual online performances from their homes, which were shown on the Symphoria website. Seeing the musicians in this new, more intimate light may have been a bonus for many.

Another silver lining to the COVID cloud occurred when the Feng family offered the orchestra the use of Inspiration Hall. The Feng family had long been patrons of Syracuse's orchestras, and Michael Feng sat on Symphoria's board. In 2010, the Fengs purchased the vacant St. Peter's Roman Catholic Church building on James Street, across the street from their family business, Progressive Expert Consulting. They renovated the building and renamed it Inspiration Hall. When COVID forced Symphoria into lockdown, the Fengs offered to let the orchestra use the space rent free as a practice and performance site. They added sound treatments to the old building and lengthened the stage at Symphoria's request. They also loaned their livestream equipment so the orchestra could sell tickets to online concerts. Symphoria performed 85 concerts at Inspiration Hall and continues to use it for Kids' Series. "That first full year of COVID, Inspiration Hall was our home," said Symphoria's executive director, Pamela Murchison. "We don't want to think where we would be without it."

"Symphoria wanted to create a welcoming space where all members of the community belong," said Pamela Murchison, explaining how Symphoria's community engagement coordinator, Lara Mosby, worked with social service agencies during the pandemic to help them feel a greater sense of belonging to the musical family. Mosby created individual plans with each organization to allow them access. Working with the Q Center, which provides a safe and supportive space for LGBTQIA+ persons and their families, Mosby arranged for them to attend a masterworks concert, streamed from Inspiration Hall, by renowned pianist Sara Davis Buechner. She then arranged for a private Zoom conversation with Buechner and the Q Center at which Buechner spoke candidly about living as a trans woman, her passion for music, the people in her life who made a difference, and so much more. The Q Center members were also introduced to the rarely heard Overture in C by Fanny Mendelssohn.

As schools went online or closed altogether due to the pandemic, teaching music became a challenge. Symphoria musicians adopted new ways of bringing music to young learners. They began a residency for third graders in the Syracuse City School District. During third grade, students transition from learning to read to reading to learn. "If they fall behind now, that can affect how they learn and how well they learn for the rest of school and the rest of their lives," the musicians said, explaining the motivation behind their Artists in Residence program. Their program was based on research that indicated that musically trained children have better reading comprehension skills. In another option, Symphoria musicians taught second, third, and fourth graders in the Syracuse City School District the basics of playing an instrument of their choice. The partnership began at the Syracuse Academy of Science with a concert, followed by an instrument petting zoo, which allowed students and their families see the possibilities. Symphoria provided the staff to teach students one of the following instruments: flute, clarinet, saxophone, trumpet, trombone, violin, and cello.

To thank the residents of the Hawley-Green Historic District, which was home to its rehearsals and concerts during COVID, Symphoria's Fall Fest brought food trucks, live performances, ice cream, and Otto the Orange to the neighborhood for a celebration outside Inspiration Hall, where later in the evening the full orchestra performed the first Spark series concert of the season. The street fest featured dances from Poised, Gifted, and Ready; guitarists from the Brady Faith Center; and ensembles from the Symphoria Youth Orchestras and the Symphoria String Quartet. "We launched this season with a Spark concert and festival in order to show appreciation to the people of the neighborhood where Symphoria concerts were filmed last year and where we will continue to perform for several months more," Pamela Murchison, Symphoria's executive director, explained. "Residents of Hawley-Green told us how much they loved the events in their neighborhood."

Location, location, location. While most orchestras perform in concert halls, Symphoria decided to experiment with different locales. Its *Harvest Moon* concert was held in Skaneateles at the beautiful Welch Allyn Lodge. Under conductor Heather Buchman, it paired rustic music of the country with locally sourced seasonal food and drink. At the *Motion Dynamics* Spark series concert, CirqOvation presented jugglers, aerial acts, and other circus performers perfectly suited to perform at the Museum of Science and Technology. As predicted by Symphoria music director Lawrence Loh, audiences gasped with wonder and delight at this unusual pairing of physicality and musicianship.

Symphoria showcased collaboration, connection, and community when it melded music, message, and meaning for the performance of a new work by local composer and Setnor School professor Joseph Downing. No performance site was more appropriate or beautiful than Syracuse's Cathedral of the Immaculate Conception for a performance of *Credo*, a work that celebrated the region's rich choral heritage. The orchestra shared the magnificent setting with the Syracuse University Oratorio Society and the combined choirs of six Syracuse churches, conducted by John Warren. Part of an innovative performance series called Time & Place, supported by the New York State Council on the Arts, *Credo* was one of five original compositions presented for the first time in public performances in beautiful iconic settings that reflect the "landscape of place" along Syracuse's Connective Corridor—a new green streetscape and cultural district in the city. The intent of the series was to create relationships between artists, the university, and community groups through a collaborative initiative that used an innovative engagement model to develop new content and reach new audiences.

The New York State Fairgrounds is not a traditional venue for orchestral music, but Symphoria again wanted to try something new. A CirqOvation concert had proven quite successful in this agricultural site, so the orchestra tried another visually interesting program with the goal of proving to the public that orchestral music did not have to be "stodgy." A mesmerizing performance of Igor Stravinsky's *Firebird Suite* with puppets from the Open Hand Theater and students and actors from the Redhouse Arts Theater in happy collaboration with Symphoria attracted a young and enthusiastic audience to a show that combined puppetry, stilting, song, orchestra, and dance. The addition of popcorn helped convince attendees that going to a symphony concert could be as much fun as going to the circus or the movies.

St. Paul's Episcopal Cathedral was the setting for Symphoria's Casual Series, which provided a more intimate concert experience in which soloists and conductors interacted directly with the audience. Concerts took place on Sunday afternoons, and guests could connect with musicians during an informal meet-and-greet immediately following the performance. The musical selections include works by underrepresented composers performed by talented local musicians. A recent casual concert called *Baroque and Neo Baroque* featured two Baroque works: the Vivaldi Concerto for Two Trumpets, with Symphoria trumpet players John Raschella and Roy Smith, and the *Overture to Cephale et Procris* by Élisabeth Jacquet de La Guerre, possibly the first woman ever to have an opera performed in France. The remainder of the concert featured works that looked back to the Baroque but with their own sense of sound and style, including Holst's *Fugal Concerto* featuring Symphoria flutist Xue Su and oboist Jillian Honn.

In big cities, orchestras are often seen as part of the cultural milieu. In Central New York, the connection between the orchestra and its audiences is very different. Symphoria sees itself as a community connector, declaring that "great music connects us as community members, at every age and in every walk of life. From Brahms to Broadway, and from movie scores to Mozart, Symphoria performances will inspire you." Fancy dress and velvet seats do not characterize either audience or venue in Syracuse. But the joy of music is the same, no matter what one wears or where one sits.

In a city noted for its sports fanaticism, turnout for Symphoria concerts is nonetheless incredibly large. Long, dreary Syracuse winters are characterized by 10 feet of snow annually. Perhaps that is why summer is so greatly appreciated and outdoor summer performances draw thousands of concertgoers of all ages who find that the music enhances their experience of the delights of warm weather and patriotic celebrations. The annual July concert series, performed throughout the six-county region, was a particularly valued summer musical experience.

Symphoria's musicians focused on maintaining a diverse audience. Rural communities generally do not have live, professional-caliber symphonic music within easy reach. "There are people for whom the concept of coming downtown to a concert hall, getting dressed up and listening to an orchestral piece may be completely foreign," Jon Garland noted. "They might not know what to wear, or when to clap if it's a multi-movement piece. The idea of sitting still and listening to music for a few hours might not be appealing." So Symphoria went to them. And it is clear that the orchestra was well received.

Reaching another underserved population and harnessing the power of music to do good, Symphoria musicians performed in oncology and dialysis treatment centers and long-term care settings through its Healing Harmonies Program. Recognition of the power of live music was growing among medical professionals and therapists because of its ability to enhance the overall patient experience. Live music in health care settings has been shown to have a positive effect on patients' anxiety, blood pressure, and heart rate. Symphoria brought live music with therapeutic benefits directly to patients who otherwise would have been unable to attend a symphony concert due to their physical challenges.

Symphoria's educational programs enriched the lives of Central New York schoolchildren by presenting dozens of performances through its education and outreach programs. Two programs were offered at Inspiration Hall, one with author Bruce Coville and a second, The Orchestra Sings, in collaboration with Carnegie Hall's LinkUp program. A third program, titled The Sound of Nature, developed in collaboration with middle school teachers and faculty from the State University of New York (SUNY) College of Environmental Science and Forestry, explored the local ecosystem through music in a STEAM-inspired program. The Kids' Series also provided three performances on Saturday mornings at Inspiration Hall, which included interactive elements and pre-concert activities.

Symphoria considers diversity, equity, and inclusion (DEI) to be drivers of institutional excellence. Symphoria's commitment is demonstrated by working with extraordinary guest artists of all ages and backgrounds. The orchestra also programs works from composers of color as well as other underrepresented groups, including women from past generations and the LGBTQIA+ community. Tai Murray is but one of many world-class artists regularly invited to perform with Symphoria.

Symphoria had asserted that "as an American orchestra in the 21st century, we consider diversity, equity, and inclusion to be drivers of institutional excellence," and added, "We recognize that this is ever-evolving work that requires attention, investment, and commitment at all levels of our organization, and we embrace this responsibility." As it looks to the future, Symphoria is hoping that it can draw on the deep commitment in the Central New York community for orchestral music making to enhance and expand its work in a DEI space.

Music director Lawrence Loh says that Symphoria's process of program planning involves musicians, conductors, community members, and administrators who explore possibilities for content and guest artists, with everyone offering ideas and having input. "We set out to plan a season that is reflective of our community," he says. "We feature exciting music from all around the world, from centuries ago to the current year. I'm particularly proud that our seasons include many composers from a wide variety of backgrounds and cultures. This gives us a vast array of artistic points of view to offer our audiences. The bottom line is that it is all great music."

Symphoria's commitment to diversity, equity, and inclusiveness is reflected in its programming. Its concerts included works by Coleridge-Taylor Perkinson, an African American composer who fused jazz, dance, pop, and orchestral music with elements of blues, spirituals, and Black folk music, and by Florence Price, the famous African American orchestral composer, pianist, organist, and music teacher. One program was devoted to the queens of soul, with music made famous by the reigning divas of soul and R&B—Aretha Franklin, Tina Turner, and Whitney Houston. Jazz vocalist Denzal Sinclaire (above) presented the music of Nat King Cole, and pianist Awadagin Pratt (below) joined Symphoria to perform Beethoven's Fourth Piano Concerto.

The Symphony Orchestra Institute has said that "musician involvement increases the effectiveness of symphony organizations," adding that "it seems that the direction, nature, and degree of musician involvement is—and is likely to be for some time—the most central issue many symphony orchestras will face." As a musician-founded and -run orchestra, Symphoria is unique but not alone. In the United Kingdom, the London Symphony Orchestra has been musician-led since its founding in 1904. Both the Vienna Philharmonic and the Berlin Philharmonic were also founded by musicians. In the United States, only the Louisiana Philharmonic and Symphoria are controlled by musicians. In all of these organizations, the orchestra's boards and staff are broadly populated by musicians. As voting members of the organization's governing body, musicians have the ability to steer the orchestra's strategic direction, make policy decisions, hire the orchestra and music directors, and develop and approve the budget.

It has been said that every orchestra oscillates between crisis and survival. Certainly, this has been true of orchestras in Central New York. What gives hope to those who love and champion orchestral music is the innovative spirit, both in organizational form and in artistic production, which infuses the work of Symphoria. As it celebrates its 10th anniversary, Symphoria is governed by a board deeply committed to its mission and its organizational and operational model, which is strongly linked to the orchestra through its firsthand grounding in music. Board president Mary Ann Tyszko (left), for example, studied mandolin and piano, sang in choruses, and is a director of her church choir. "Serving on Symphoria's Board of Directors gives me a chance to combine my love of music and my skills in development in the hometown I love," says Tyszko. Four members of the orchestra are board members (Amy Christian, Kelly Covert, Jon Garland, and Gregory Wood), as is its program annotator, Peter Rabinowitz. Having a board that is so in tune with the orchestra's mission, vision, and purpose intentionality assures that Symphoria will not suffer the fate of its many predecessors.

Audience engagement is vital to Symphoria's future. The orchestra is trying to engage its constituents in ways that are relevant and valuable while being cognizant of the challenges of building an audience that is more reflective of the demographics of the community. Spark series concerts are specifically designed with this goal in mind. They are offered in different venues, are played in sets, allow people to walk around and mingle with one another, and offer food. Built into Symphoria's Casual series are informal meet-and-greets with musicians and conductors after each performance. These sessions, hosted by the generous volunteers at St. Paul's Episcopal Church, give audience members the opportunity to interact with each other and to ask composers and musicians questions about the music that was performed. Stepping out of the world created on the stage to join with the audience on an intimate basis helps to develop relationships between patrons and their orchestra, strengthening the bonds between audience and musicians in a way that is welcoming rather than intimidating. They also offer the community a different view of its orchestra, one that is committed to bettering the community and its residents.

The successful orchestra of the 21st century has to reach out to the broader community, engage with it, and enable its members to experience the joy of orchestral performance. Musicians have to share their joy in performance with new audiences, in new venues, and with new repertoire. They have to work collaboratively with other community organizations, and they have to play a significant role in the governance of the orchestra with which they perform. This is the playbook that Symphoria has put into practice. Symphoria's music director, Lawrence Loh, noted that "from the very beginning, our musicians strongly committed to play an active role in every aspect of what we do as an organization, far beyond performing music on the stage. Symphoria will always strive to be a vital part of the cultural, educational, social and economic life of Syracuse and we are absolutely dedicated to that mission. Onward, Symphoria!"

Bibliography

Arian, Edward. *Bach, Beethoven, and Bureaucracy: The Case of the Philadelphia Orchestra*. Tuscaloosa: University of Alabama Press, 1971.

Bruce, Dwight H. *Memorial History of Syracuse, N.Y., from Its Settlement to the Present Time*. Syracuse: H.P. Smith & Company, 1891.

Flanagan, Robert J. *The Perilous Life of Symphony Orchestras: Artistic Triumphs and Economic Challenges*. New Haven: Yale University Press, 2012.

Kaiser, Linda Pembroke. *Pulling Strings: The Legacy of Melville A. Clark*. Syracuse: Syracuse University Press, 2010.

Larson, Susan W. *A History of Symphony Orchestras in Syracuse New York from 1848 to 1969*. Syracuse University master's thesis, 2010.

Newton, Travis. *Symphonic Music in Central New York: A Time of Change and Uncertainty*. Original case study by the author.

ABOUT THE ONONDAGA HISTORICAL ASSOCIATION

Historic perspective adds value—it makes everything more interesting and provides depth, substance, and meaning. It instills pride and helps create a determination to build and leave legacies that are worthy of our great heritage. It enhances judgment in planning our future and helps develop a more optimistic attitude about that future. Pride in place, determination to improve the present, and optimism about the future all have their foundations in our past. The Onondaga Historical Association (OHA) has always believed that our shared collective history is the foundation for our future together and continues to remain as dedicated to that concept today as it has been for over 153 years.

The OHA's Richard & Carolyn Wright Research Center, located on the second floor of the OHA building in downtown Syracuse, houses the community's largest collection of local history—one it has been continually aggregating for a century and a half. The collection includes some of the most important historical research material in the country and is an invaluable resource for all those who study our community's past. The OHA has grown over the years to become more than just a repository and a museum. Today, it offers research and educational services, retail operations, the Skä•nonh—Great Law of Peace Center, the St. Marie Among the Iroquois Mission site museum, the Brewseum at Heritage Hill, and countless exhibits throughout the community. The OHA continues to grow in order to preserve and tell the stories of Onondaga County's history.

Like Symphoria, the Onondaga Historical Association is dedicated to making Central New York and its diverse cultural heritage a place of excellence and to fulfill its vision "to instill pride in place and identity, to create a determination to build and leave legacies that are worthy of our great heritage, and to provide enhanced judgment and optimism in charting a promising future."

DISCOVER THOUSANDS OF LOCAL HISTORY BOOKS FEATURING MILLIONS OF VINTAGE IMAGES

Arcadia Publishing, the leading local history publisher in the United States, is committed to making history accessible and meaningful through publishing books that celebrate and preserve the heritage of America's people and places.

Find more books like this at
www.arcadiapublishing.com

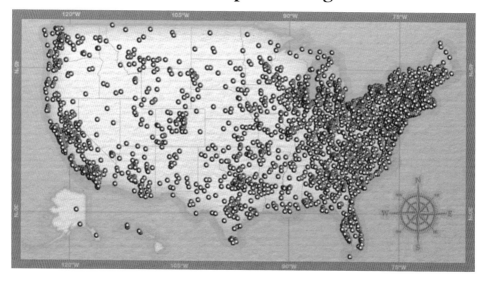

Search for your hometown history, your old stomping grounds, and even your favorite sports team.

Consistent with our mission to preserve history on a local level, this book was printed in South Carolina on American-made paper and manufactured entirely in the United States. Products carrying the accredited Forest Stewardship Council (FSC) label are printed on 100 percent FSC-certified paper.

MADE IN THE

USA